I Ha

by Mickey Daronco

I have a tan cat.

My tan cat is fat.

My cat is on the mat.

I have a can.

I put my can in a pan.

The pan is not hot yet.

I have a big bag.

My bag is red.

My red bag has a tag.

I have a fan.

I put my fan in a van.

I will go home with it.

I have a map.

I set my map on my lap.

I look at the map.

I have a bat.
I put my cap
on my bat.

I put my cap on me!